Don't You Believe It!

By Eric Metaxas
Illustrated by Marc Dennis

St. Martin's Griffin
New York

Book Design by Marc Dennis

Library of Congress Cataloging-in-Publication Data

Metaxas, Eric.
    Don't you believe it! / by Eric Metaxas and Marc Dennis.
        p. cm.
    ISBN 0-312-14319-2
    1. Ripley's believe it or not (New York:1965)—Parodies,
imitations, etc. 2. American wit and humor. I. Dennis, Marc.
II. Title.
    PN6231.P3M48 1996
    741.5'973—dc20
96-10368
                                                                    CIP

First St. Martin's Griffin Edition: July 1996

10 9 8 7 6 5 4 3 2 1

Acknowledgments

I want to take this opportunity to thank several persons. First of all **Jim Shapiro**, who shepherded the conception of it all on the steps of the Widener Library in that dastardly hot summer of '85. Man, was it hot!—eh "Jimmy"? And **Ashley Marable**—how I derided his choicest suggestions, only to realize it was I who ought to have been derided! *Mea Culpa*, Ash! And then there's **Christopher Noel**, that pseudo-shy, indefatigable kook, whose friends simply call him "Chris"—and his friend, **Matt Goodman**, who also calls him "Chris". And what about **Dr. Christopher Lennox Hanes?** Well?! And lastly, but mostly, those two inveterate Danburians, my old pal, **John Tomanio**, and my beloved brother, **John Metaxas**, without whose over-the-top sensibilities and canny suggestions this volume would be a handsome coffeetable book on whitewater rafting—or merely a crude parody of itself! And who could forget old **what's his name!** *Vielen dank, alle!*

E.M., New Canaan, Connecticut, April 1996

I dedicate this book to **Mom, Dad, Scott, Bruce, Kevin,** and **Glenn.**

M.D., New York, New York, April 1996

THE PATRIOTIC FOREST
IN Illyria, Vermont, EVERY STEP THROUGH THE FALLEN LEAVES STREWN ON THE FOREST'S FLOOR PRODUCES TONES THAT SOUND PRECISELY LIKE A *ROUSING SOUSA MARCH!*

FOUR OF THE PAGES IN THIS BOOK ARE OUT OF ORDER

LEONORA PORTER of Youngstown, Ohio, GAVE BIRTH TO ONE AND ONE-HALF SETS OF TWINS!

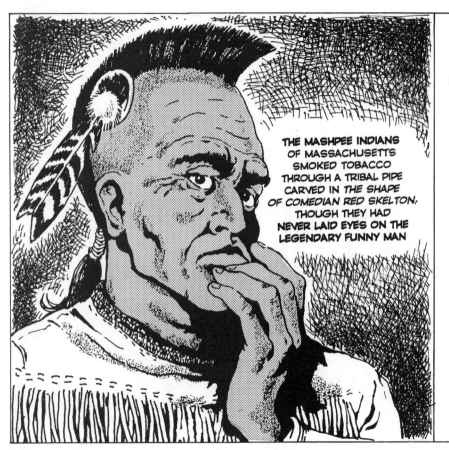

THE MASHPEE INDIANS OF MASSACHUSETTS SMOKED TOBACCO THROUGH A TRIBAL PIPE CARVED IN *THE SHAPE OF COMEDIAN RED SKELTON,* THOUGH THEY HAD NEVER LAID EYES ON THE LEGENDARY FUNNY MAN

MARK TWAIN IS NOT THE PEN NAME OF SAMUEL CLEMENS, AS IS POPULARLY BELIEVED, BUT OF ANOTHER MAN ENTIRELY WHO SHUNNED THE ATTENTION HEAPED ON HIM BY HIS MANY FANS, AND *WHO NEVER IN HIS LIFETIME WROTE A SINGLE ARTICLE, STORY, OR BOOK OF ANY KIND!*

A PET HAMSTER BELONGING TO **MARION PERRETI** of Astoria, New York LIVED IN A CHICKEN COOP AND BEHAVED SO MUCH LIKE A CHICKEN THAT IT WAS EVENTUALLY MADE INTO AN EXCELLENT CHICKEN SOUP WITH CARROTS AND ONIONS

BEDBUGS ARE NOT BUGS AT ALL, BUT A SPECIES OF BLOODWORMS THAT GORGE THEMSELVES ON MATTRESS STUFFING AND CAN GROW TO LENGTHS EXCEEDING TWO YARDS

THE CALIPH OF ANCIENT TURKESTAN (A.D. 946 - 989), COULD PART HIS HAIR WITH HIS OWN TONGUE

CAPT. JAMES COOK OF "HMS BOUNTY" FAME
WAS BLIND FROM BIRTH, BUT COULD NAVIGATE
PERFECTLY WELL USING HIS UNCANNY SENSE OF
SMELL -- HE CLAIMED THAT THE STARS SMELLED
LIKE PEACHES AND ROSE PETALS, BUT PINCHED
HIS NOSE IN DISGUST AT THE FULL MOON,
WHICH HE SAID REEKED OF FOUL BILGEWATER

SAM, A BORDER COLLIE
OWNED BY ROBERT MCREADY
of Los Alamos, New Mexico,
HAS BEEN TRAINED
TO STAY AIRBORNE
FOR HOURS AT A TIME

PRESIDENT THEODORE ROOSEVELT, IN THE HOPES OF GUARANTEEING HIMSELF IMMORTALITY, SPENT MANY HOURS SECRETLY DOODLING HIS NAME AND **CRUDE** SKETCHES OF HIMSELF INTO THE WOODWORK OF VARIOUS ROOMS THROUGHOUT THE WHITE HOUSE DURING HIS RESIDENCE THERE

THE EMPIRE STATE BUILDING in New York City,

WILL SPIN 360 DEGREES ON ITS AXIS AT THE SLIGHTEST PUSH *FROM ANY PASSERBY* — BUT IN THE MORE THAN FIFTY-YEAR HISTORY OF THE LANDMARK BUILDING *NOT A SINGLE PERSON HAS EVER BEEN BRAZEN ENOUGH TO ATTEMPT IT*

THE BREAKFAST DYNASTY

SAM EGG, of Ellsville, Missouri MARRIED LENA BACON -- THEY HAD FIVE DAUGHTERS WHOM THEY NAMED PANCAKE, FRENCH TOAST, OATMEAL, COLD CEREAL, AND WAFFLES. WAFFLES WAS THE ONLY ONE TO WED, MARRYING A FINANCIER NAMED OVER-EASY. SHE BORE HIM THREE CHILDREN WHOM THEY NAMED GRITS, HOME FRIES, AND O.J., WHO BECAME A FAMOUS RUNNINGBACK FOR THE NATIONAL FOOTBALL LEAGUE'S BUFFALO BILLS, AND WHO APPEARED ON A BOX OF *WHEATIES* BREAKFAST CEREAL!

POTATO SHAPED LIKE A CARROT

EARWIGS

HAVE NO EARS TO SPEAK OF — AND ARE DEATHLY AFRAID OF WIGS!

PERRY ENTWHISTLE
of Brookfield, New York
HAD HAIR SO THICK
NO HUMAN BARBER
WAS ABLE TO CUT IT

A GRAPEFRUIT
*THE SIZE OF
A TUMOR,*
Angel Falls, Iowa

THE **COMMON DACHSHUND**
ENTERS LIFE WITH A SHINY COAT
OF **BRILLIANT GREEN FUR**
- IT IS NOT UNTIL THE ANIMALS REACH
FULL MATURITY THAT THEY TAKE ON
THEIR CHARACTERISTIC WALNUT HUE

DAME LOUISA MAY BARTON (1845 - 1848)
PLAYED LADY MACBETH ON THE LONDON
STAGE AT AGE TWO, TO GREAT CRITICAL
AND POPULAR ACCLAIM -- SHE BESTED
THIS PERFORMANCE, HOWEVER, WHEN
SHE PLAYED OTHELLO AT TWO AND A HALF!
SHE WAS A HAS-BEEN AT AGE THREE,
AND DIED OF OLD AGE AT THREE AND A HALF!

DOROTHY JOHNSON HERRICK,
of West Eaton, Illinois,
IS THE MOTHER OF SEVEN CHILDREN
BY ELEVEN DIFFERENT HUSBANDS

FRIEDRICH NIETZSCHE,
THE FAMOUS PHILOSOPHER
AND AUTHOR, WAS IN REALITY
A PAIR OF TWINS, BORN SEVEN
MINUTES APART, EACH NAMED
FRIEDRICH, WHO MADE A
LIFELONG GAME OF
PRETENDING TO BE
THE SAME PERSON

GOLDFISH
WILL THRIVE IN
A SOLUTION OF
*SELTZER AND
TABASCO SAUCE*

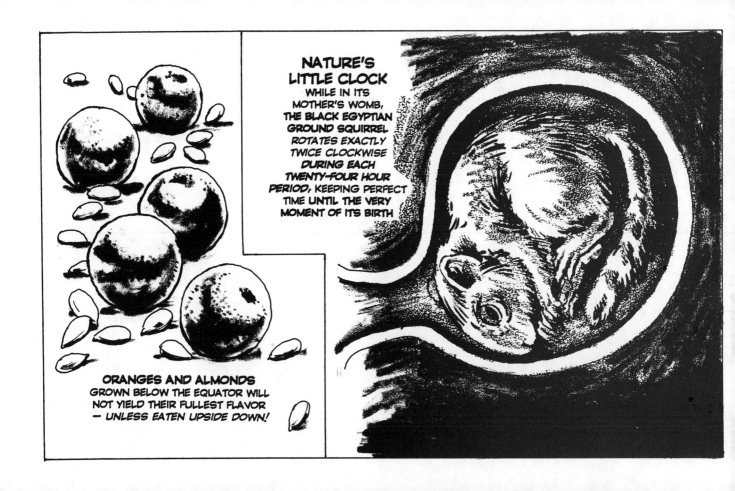

AN ELM TREE
GROWING
AROUND
A BOY,
Suffield,
Connecticut

IBO TRIBESMEN
in Nigeria
BELIEVE THAT EVERY MIRROR
ACTUALLY CONTAINS THE
INVERTED UNIVERSE IT DEPICTS!
WHEN ASKED HOW SO MANY
UNIVERSES COULD BE CONTAINED
WITHIN OUR OWN UNIVERSE
THEY SIMPLY SHRUG AND
GO ABOUT THEIR BUSINESS!

THE POPULAR ENGLISH SURNAME JOHNSON IS DERIVED FROM A CHOCTAW WORD MEANING "FIVE BOBCATS"

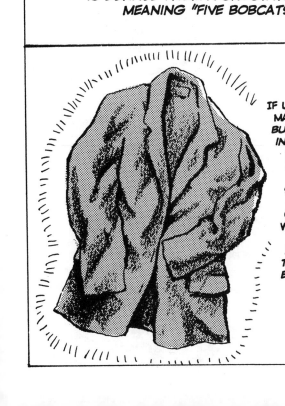

IF UNUSED FOR MANY YEARS, BUTTONHOLES IN CLOTHING MADE OF NATURAL FIBERS SUCH AS COTTON OR WOOL WILL "HEAL," LEAVING NO TRACE THEY WERE EVER THERE!

IN THE ERRONEOUS BELIEF THAT MEN FIND SUCH BEHAVIOR ATTRACTIVE, UNWED FRENCH WOMEN WILL TO THIS DAY BUG THEIR EYES OUT "FROG-FASHION" AT THE PASSING OF ELIGIBLE BACHELORS!

THE "LOCO SCHOOLMASTER," A HILL in Paxtua, Mexico GIVES TRAVELLERS WHO ASCEND TO ITS PEAK THE TEMPORARY ILLUSION OF BEING MUCH MORE EDUCATED THAN THEY ACTUALLY ARE

LEFT-HANDEDNESS AFFECTS RIGHT-HANDED PERSONS NEARLY *TWICE AS OFTEN AS IT DOES ANY OTHER GROUP*

BEFORE THE CIVIL WAR, MOST OF THE **COFFEE** DRUNK IN THE UNITED STATES WAS LIGHT BLUE IN COLOR AND EMANATED A PLEASANT, SMOKY ODOR MUCH LIKE GRILLED MEAT

IN HER LIFETIME, **MRS. HILDA MCMANUS** (1887 - 1949), of Chicago, Illinois GAVE BIRTH TO FOURTEEN CHILDREN — *NONE OF THEM IN CHRONOLOGICAL ORDER!*

THE GREAT PANDA of China SUBSISTS ALMOST ENTIRELY ON THE TENDER LEAVES OF THE BAMBOO TREE, BUT IF GIVEN HIS DRUTHERS THE CLEVER MAMMAL WILL INVARIABLY CHOOSE TO DINE ON RICH MEAT DISHES SUCH AS RAGOUTS AND STROGANOFFS — ALWAYS WASHING THEM DOWN WITH SEVERAL BOTTLES OF THE FINEST FRENCH WINES AND A STEAMING POT OF FRESHLY BREWED COFFEE!

WAITER, THERE'S A HAIR IN MY APPLE

ORCHARD KEEPERS in Lisseburg, Switzerland HAVE LONG
TOLD THE STORY OF THE GOLDEN-HAIRED MAIDEN
WHOSE HEART WAS BROKEN WHEN THE YOUNG SWAIN
WHO HAD PROPOSED TO HER INFORMED HER THAT HE
WAS IN LOVE WITH AN ACTRESS IN THE FAR-AWAY CITY
OF BASEL. LEGEND HAS IT THAT AFTER HE DEPARTED
THE FAIR-HAIRED MAIDEN PINED AWAY IN THE COOL
SHADE OF THE HOARY TREE NEAR HER FATHER'S FARM,
WHERE SHE AND HER LOST LOVE HAD SPENT THE
BLISSFUL DAYS OF THEIR ARDOR. SHE DIED OF HER
GRIEF SOME MONTHS AFTERWARD, AND WAS BURIED,
ACCORDING TO HER WISHES, BENEATH THE ANCIENT
TREE. TO THIS VERY DAY THE YELLOW APPLES FROM
THAT TREE ARE PRIZED THROUGHOUT SWITZERLAND FOR
THEIR EXTRAORDINARY BEAUTY...AND AT THE CENTER OF
EACH OF THEM — WITHOUT FAIL — *IS FOUND A SINGLE,
COILED STRAND OF BEAUTIFUL GOLDEN HAIR*

VOLTAIRE (1694 - 1778), THE FAMED FRENCH PHILOSOPHER AND AUTHOR, KEPT A WILD GOAT AS A COMPANION FOR THIRTY YEARS. HE CLAIMED THE ANIMAL WROTE MUCH OF THE TEXT OF HIS NOVEL *CANDIDE*, AND WHEN THE BOOK WAS GOING TO PRESS, THE GOAT PROOFREAD IT LINE BY LINE —*ALTHOUGH LEGALLY BLIND AT THE TIME!*

A U.S. DIME IN THE SIZE AND SHAPE OF A QUARTER

A BENT SPOON BEARING THE PERMANENT IMAGE OF ISRAELI PSYCHIC URI GELLER, Acton, Ohio

THE FAMOUSLY
SLOW ELEVATORS
IN THE LANDMARK
FLATIRON BUILDING
of New York City
WERE INSTALLED
AND FULLY
OPERATIONAL
IN 1888
— FIFTEEN YEARS
BEFORE
CONSTRUCTION
OF THE BUILDING
ITSELF WAS BEGUN!

THE TENDER FLESH
OF MONARCH BUTTERFLIES
SMELLS EXACTLY LIKE
FRESH PEPPERONI

CHECKS SIGNED
AT THE STROKE
OF MIDNIGHT
ARE NOT VALID

TANU, A PET GOAT
IN THE VILLAGE of Murai, Uganda, IS THE LEGAL GUARDIAN TO EACH OF THE VILLAGES 78 INHABITANTS -- SHE ROSE TO THIS POSITION THROUGH A SERIES OF MANEUVERS SO STUNNINGLY MACHIAVELLIAN IN THEIR NATURE THAT THE ENTIRE REGION WAS TURNED UPSIDE DOWN — AND ALL WHO OPPOSED HER LOST THEIR LIVES

MANY OF THE NATIVES on the island of MADAGASCAR HAVE NO ANCESTORS

LADY EMMELINE,
THE FRENCH PLAYWRIGHT, SO IDENTIFIED WITH HER IDOL, THE GREAT WILLIAM SHAKESPEARE, THAT WHENEVER SHE READ ANY PART OF HIS PLAYS SHE WOULD *TEMPORARILY APPEAR BALDHEADED*

IN MANY MUSLIM NATIONS, PREMATURE BALDNESS IS TAKEN AS A LEGAL ADMISSION OF GUILT

THE HUMAN FILLET!
UPON REACHING MATURITY, THE BODY OF SIR THEDRIC (1235 - 1284), *THE BONELESS KNIGHT,* LOST ALL TRACE OF A SKELETON -- FROM THAT POINT ON HE REFUSED TO REMOVE HIS SUIT OF ARMOR, WHICH SERVED AS A TRUSTY EXOSKELETON, *MAKING HIM THE ONLY RECORDED CRUSTACEAN IN HUMAN HISTORY!*

ITALIAN FOOD, AS WE KNOW IT, WAS INVENTED IN CHINA

DURING THE SEVERE MIDWESTERN FLOODS OF 1871, THE PARCHED STATE OF KANSAS SWELLED TO NEARLY TWICE ITS SIZE

NEARLY NINE-TENTHS OF THE WORLD'S CHOCOLATE CONSUMPTION IS ATTRIBUTED TO POLICE CAPTAINS

EARRINGS PRECEDED EARS BY TWO CENTURIES

THE ONONDAGA INDIANS of North America
GAVE THE WORLD ITS VERY FIRST BRIDGES WHEN THEY DISCOVERED
THEY COULD SIMPLY MAKE THEIR BIRCH BARK CANOES LONG ENOUGH
TO SPAN ANY WATERWAY! SOME OF THESE AMAZING VESSELS ARE
OVER HALF A MILE LONG AND IF USED AS CONVENTIONAL CANOES
WOULD EACH REQUIRE AS MANY AS *SEVEN HUNDRED PADDLING BRAVES!*

MITHRADATES II,
RULER OF PERSIA, HAD SUCH A NOTORIOUS
SWEET TOOTH THAT HE WOULD QUAFF SEVERAL
BARRELS OF *PURE HONEY* AT EVERY MEAL --
THE SWEET SUBSTANCE MADE HIM SO THIRSTY
THAT HE WOULD ALWAYS WASH IT DOWN WITH
SEVERAL BARRELSFUL OF A THICK LIQUID
— THAT WAS ALSO *100% PURE HONEY!*

OAK TREE THAT GREW THROUGH A LIVE ELEPHANT

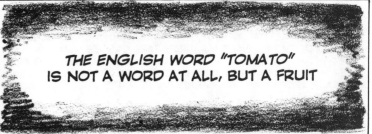

THE ENGLISH WORD "TOMATO" IS NOT A WORD AT ALL, BUT A FRUIT

AN INSECT ORCHESTRA

EMMETT DULLES of Erie, Pennsylvania TRAINED TWENTY-FIVE BEETLES, SIX HORSEFLIES AND SIX MOSQUITOES TO PLAY THE STAR SPANGLED BANNER — BACKWARDS!

MOST FOREST FIRES
ARE CAUSED BY MICE
-- THE RODENTS SMEAR
THEMSELVES WITH
THE RESIN FROM PINE
TREES AND RUN
THROUGH CAMPFIRES
BEFORE ANYONE
CAN STOP THEM

VANDERHOEVEN

AUGUST VANDERHOEVEN,
A FOOT-SOLDIER IN THE BOER WAR,
WAS SHOT AND KILLED BY A BULLET
THAT ACTUALLY HAD HIS NAME ON IT

HERMAN MELVILLE, WHILE
WRITING HIS GREAT NOVEL
"MOBY DICK," LIVED ON A DIET
CONSISTING OF NOTHING BUT
RAW FISH AND STRAINED KRILL,
AND DAILY WOULD TAKE A WALK
AROUND HIS NEIGHBORHOOD
WHILE WEARING AN ELABORATE
PAPIER-MACHE WHALE COSTUME.
HIS NEIGHBOR, THE ESSAYIST
RALPH WALDO EMERSON, SO
FEARED "THIS MONSTROUS
STROLLING WHALENESS" THAT HE
COWERED IN HIS ROOT CELLAR
WHENEVER MELVILLE APPEARED!

WORLD'S SMALLEST JAIL
THE TOWN JAIL in Las Mujeres, Mexico, IS NO BIGGER THAN A STANDARD CIGAR BOX — YET IT SUPPORTS A STAFF OF EIGHT FULL-TIME PERSONS AND *CONTAINS A DIMINUTIVE KITCHEN, LIBRARY AND SPORTS FACILITY*

A SQUARE CIRCLE,
DRAWN BY
JAMES ESTERHAZY
Plymouth, Massachusetts

ARMAND LEWIS of Cooperville, Maine
— KNOWN AS "THE DOWNEAST BEAU BRUMMELL" — DID NOT CONSIDER HIMSELF FULLY DRESSED UNTIL *HE PUT ON A SMART-LOOKING "BEARD" OF LIVING SPIDERS* -- THE EIGHT-LEGGED CREATURES WOULD REMAIN PERFECTLY MOTIONLESS ON LEWIS' CHIN AND JOWLS WHILE HE CONDUCTED HIS DAILY AFFAIRS — AND WERE ALWAYS RETIRED TO THEIR MASON JAR AT THE *PRECISE STROKE OF MIDNIGHT!*

JANE JACOBS,
of Holmdel, New Jersey,
WHILE SWEEPING
HER LIVINGROOM,
FOUND A DUST BALL
IN THE COMPELLING
LIKENESS OF
*A DIMINUTIVE
BEARDED MAN
WEARING
EYEGLASSES!*

A SWEATHOG MOUNT RUSHMORE

ERNIE SYZSNIK, A DEVOTED FAN OF THE '70S HIT TELEVISION SITCOM "WELCOME BACK, KOTTER," IS PROCEEDING WITH PLANS TO CREATE A MT. RUSHMORE-SIZED SCULPTURE OF THE FOUR ACTORS WHO PLAYED THE BELOVED "SWEATHOGS" ON THE SHOW. THEIR MENTOR, MR. KOTTER, PLAYED BY GABE KAPLAN, WILL ALSO BE FEATURED, ALTHOUGH THUS FAR NO PLANS HAVE BEEN MADE TO INCLUDE THE SCHOOL'S PRINCIPAL, MR. WOODMAN.

A COMMON
BOLL WEEVIL
ADOPTED
AND NURSED
A TABBY CAT,
OWNED BY
LUCAS BENNETT
England, 1918

PTU!

ERNEST "SPITZ" HAMMER, of Tupelo, Michigan, EARNED HIS CHEEKY SOBRIQUET FOR THE ABILITY TO "SIGN" HIS NAME ON A WALL AT TWENTY PACES BY *EXPECTORATING*

THE DESERT FOX
FIELD MARSHALL *ERWIN ROMMEL* OF THE NAZI FORCES WAS A PRACTICED WORDSMITH AND SUPERSTITIOUSLY REFUSED TO LEAVE HIS TENT IN THE MORNING *BEFORE COMPOSING A DIFFICULT ACROSTIC AND WORD JUMBLE* FOR THAT MORNING'S FIELD REPORT

CATCH-22!

BECAUSE THE EYES OF THE **ASIAN SPROUL FLIES** ARE LOCATED UNDER THEIR WINGS, THE POOR CREATURES CANNOT SEE UNLESS THEY ARE IN FLIGHT — YET THEY DON'T DARE FLY SINCE *THEY CAN'T SEE WHAT'S AROUND THEM UNTIL THEY ARE ACTUALLY FLYING!*

THERESA BARNUM COULD WHISPER THE ENTIRE TEXT TO THE DECLARATION OF INDEPENDENCE AND JUGGLE INDIAN CLUBS *WHILE TREADING WATER IN BOILING RAPIDS!*

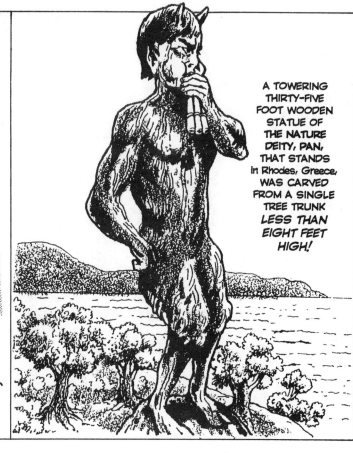

A TOWERING THIRTY-FIVE FOOT WOODEN STATUE OF THE NATURE DEITY, PAN, THAT STANDS in Rhodes, Greece, WAS CARVED FROM A SINGLE TREE TRUNK *LESS THAN EIGHT FEET HIGH!*

WHEN IN FLIGHT, MOST BIRDS CONTAIN NO SUBATOMIC PARTICLES WHATEVER

ON HIS FABLED "NEVERLAND" RANCH, ECCENTRIC POP SINGER **MICHAEL JACKSON** KEEPS THREE RETIRED U.S. POSTAL WORKERS AS "PETS"

PAUL BUNYAN, THE LEGENDARY LUMBERJACK OF FOLKLORE, WAS AN ACTUAL MAN WHO NEVER FELLED A TREE, NEVER SWUNG AN AXE, DID NOT HAVE A BLUE OX NAMED BABE, AND WAS NOT, IN FACT, NAMED PAUL AT ALL — NEITHER WAS HIS LAST NAME BUNYAN!

A CHICKEN EGG IN THE SHAPE OF THE TAJ MAHAL

A GLUTTON FOR PUNISHMENT
THE VORACIOUS *CANNIBAL SHREW* of West Africa IS SO GREEDY WHEN IT COMES TO FOOD THAT *IT WILL SOMETIMES FINISH A MEAL BY EATING ITSELF!*

THE MISSOURI INKBUSH BEARS POTENT BERRIES THAT WERE USED BY THE PLAINS INDIANS TO MAKE INKS AND DYES OF VARIOUS COLORS -- SO POTENT ARE THESE EXTRAORDINARY FRUITS THAT A SINGLE PEA-SIZED BERRY MAKES ENOUGH INK *TO DYE THE SURFACE OF EVERY SINGLE PLANET IN THE KNOWN UNIVERSE MANY TIMES OVER!*

CALVERT MORGAN (1688 - 1751), A MINISTER IN THE CHURCH OF ENGLAND, HAD MEMORIZED THE ENTIRE OLD TESTAMENT SCRIPTURES IN THE ORIGINAL HEBREW BY THE AGE OF FOUR YEARS -- BUT BY THE TIME HE WAS SIX HE HAD FORGOTTEN EVERY WORD — AND BY EIGHT HE WAS *ROBBING STAGECOACHES*

INDIAN FAKIRS CAN SNEEZE BACKWARDS

KIOSKS
in Quito, Ecuador's capitol city, HAVE BEEN SUCCESSFULLY OWNED AND OPERATED BY NATIVE SPIDER MONKEYS FOR MANY GENERATIONS

HANNIBAL DID NOT CROSS THE ALPS ON ELEPHANTS, AS IS POPULARLY BELIEVED, BUT ON HORSES SO OBESE THAT THE AMUSED LOCALS DERISIVELY DUBBED THEM "ELEFANTI" — THUS THE CRUEL MISTAKE OF POSTERITY

PENNY FOR YOUR THOUGHTS

THE MAN WHOSE PROFILE APPEARS ON THE ONE-CENT COIN *IS NOT ABRAHAM LINCOLN,* AS IS POPULARLY BELIEVED, BUT A PRACTICAL JOKESTER NAMED POMPEI McFIBB, WHO BORE SUCH AN UNCANNY RESEMBLANCE TO THE 16TH PRESIDENT THAT HE WAS ABLE TO FOOL THE SCULPTORS EVERY TIME! McFIBB ALSO APPEARS IN THE LINCOLN MEMORIAL AND ON MT. RUSHMORE! IN EACH CASE THE COST TO TAXPAYERS WAS TOO PROHIBITIVE TO ALLOW THE WORK TO BE REDONE, SO *THESE ERRORS STAND TO THIS DAY AS SOBERING MONUMENTS TO ONE MAN'S MISPLACED SENSE OF HUMOR*

THE UNITED NATIONS
GENERAL CONSULATE
BUILDING, LOCATED
in New York City,
RESTS ON A VAST SLAB
OF MARSHMALLOWS

GENERAL CYRUS CHOKE
IN 1860 PRODUCED A PATENT
FOR A STEAM-DRIVEN HAIRPIECE

LORD MELMAN,
THE FOURTH ARCHDUKE
OF CORNWALL,
HAD A COUGH THAT SOUNDED
LIKE A SNEEZE, AND A SNEEZE
THAT SOUNDED LIKE A COUGH.
HE WORE ALL HIS UNDERWEAR
BACKWARDS, WHISTLED THROUGH
HIS NOSE, AND STOOD ON HIS
HANDS THROUGHOUT THE ENTIRE
*FOUR-HOUR CORONATION OF
QUEEN ELIZABETH*

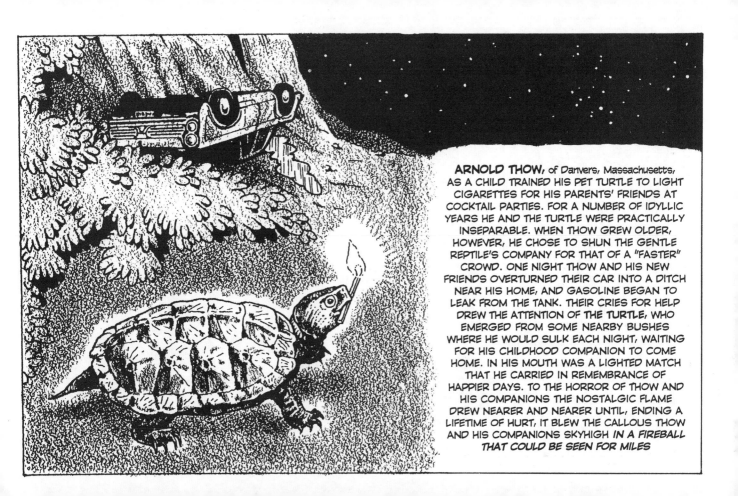

ARNOLD THOW, of Danvers, Massachusetts, AS A CHILD TRAINED HIS PET TURTLE TO LIGHT CIGARETTES FOR HIS PARENTS' FRIENDS AT COCKTAIL PARTIES. FOR A NUMBER OF IDYLLIC YEARS HE AND THE TURTLE WERE PRACTICALLY INSEPARABLE. WHEN THOW GREW OLDER, HOWEVER, HE CHOSE TO SHUN THE GENTLE REPTILE'S COMPANY FOR THAT OF A "FASTER" CROWD. ONE NIGHT THOW AND HIS NEW FRIENDS OVERTURNED THEIR CAR INTO A DITCH NEAR HIS HOME, AND GASOLINE BEGAN TO LEAK FROM THE TANK. THEIR CRIES FOR HELP DREW THE ATTENTION OF **THE TURTLE,** WHO EMERGED FROM SOME NEARBY BUSHES WHERE HE WOULD SULK EACH NIGHT, WAITING FOR HIS CHILDHOOD COMPANION TO COME HOME. IN HIS MOUTH WAS A LIGHTED MATCH THAT HE CARRIED IN REMEMBRANCE OF HAPPIER DAYS. TO THE HORROR OF THOW AND HIS COMPANIONS THE NOSTALGIC FLAME DREW NEARER AND NEARER UNTIL, ENDING A LIFETIME OF HURT, IT BLEW THE CALLOUS THOW AND HIS COMPANIONS SKYHIGH *IN A FIREBALL THAT COULD BE SEEN FOR MILES*

SCIENCE TEACHES US THAT ONE OUT OF EVERY THOUSAND WATERFALLS *RUNS BACKWARDS AS WELL AS FORWARDS*

MAYAN KINGS
DURING THE MONTHS OF SUMMER WOULD EAT NOTHING BUT POPCORN IN THE HOPES THAT THE CRACKLY DELICACY WOULD ENABLE THEM TO LOSE WEIGHT AND ONCE AGAIN RULE THEIR SUBJECTS WITHOUT FEAR OF SUCH DERISIVE EPITHETS AS *"YOUR ROYAL TUBBINESS"* AND *"MOST LUMINOUS FATSO"*

THOUGH **BENJAMIN FRANKLIN** NEVER WORE A WIG, HE IS KNOWN TO HAVE SMEARED WIG ADHESIVES ON HIS PATE WHILE PERFORMING HIS TOILETTE, BELIEVING THE SMELL WAS EFFECTIVE IN DRIVING AWAY GOBLINS AND UNRULY CHILDREN

LAUREL BANNISTER of Oakwood, Arkansas HAS TWO MASTER'S DEGREES, YET CANNOT SEEM TO FIND A JOB IN HER OWN FIELD -- SHE HAS WORKED AS A TEACHER AND WAITRESS SOME, THOUGH THE PAY IS NOT GREAT -- SHE ALSO HAS YET TO FIND A MAN THAT SUITS HER!

RASPBERRY HILL, A PICTURESQUE HAMLET in Coventry, England, DID NOT GET ITS NAME FROM THE MANY GAILY-COLORED RASPBERRY BUSHES THAT DOT ITS COUNTRY LANES AND MEADOWS— BUT FROM THE RUDE "RASPBERRY" SOUNDS WITH WHICH ITS BOORISH INHABITANTS *REGULARLY GREET EACH OTHER*

SQUIRTING DAGGER FOUND IN THE RUINS OF ANCIENT ASSYRIA

PAPER WAS FIRST USED AS SOMETHING TO PUT UNDER ROCKS AND OTHER HEAVY DECORATIVE OBJECTS -- IT WAS NOT UNTIL AN EGYPTIAN SCRIBE WAS CASTING ABOUT FOR SOMETHING UPON WHICH TO TRANSCRIBE SOME **GRAIN AND OAT ACCOUNTS** THAT HE SAW THE APPROPRIATENESS OF THE "PAPER." SINCE THAT TIME PAPER HAS BEEN THE CHIEF WAY PEOPLE OF ALL COUNTRIES HAVE RECORDED THEIR IDEAS

THE FIRST **LOCOMOTIVE TRAINS** *DID NOT RUN ON TRACKS AND WERE DRAWN BY VAST TEAMS OF HORSES — SOMETIMES NUMBERING IN THE THOUSANDS*

THE **KALI TRIBESMEN** of Southern Pakistan, *HAVE LUNGS SO POWERFUL THEY ARE ABLE TO APPLY THEIR LIPS TO AN INCH-THICK PLANK OF LUMBER AND BLOW BUBBLES OF SOLID WOOD*

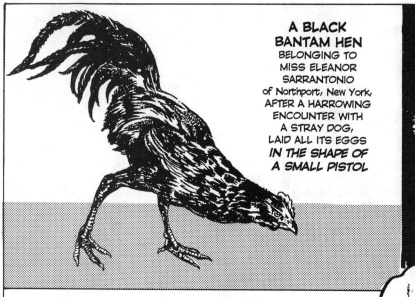

A BLACK BANTAM HEN BELONGING TO MISS ELEANOR SARRANTONIO of Northport, New York, AFTER A HARROWING ENCOUNTER WITH A STRAY DOG, LAID ALL ITS EGGS *IN THE SHAPE OF A SMALL PISTOL*

"UNCLE WIGGY"

JAMES ELMORE, A LOBSTERMAN of Edgartown, Massachusetts HAS WORN THE SAME OUTRAGEOUS WIG EVERY DAY WITHOUT EXCEPTION FOR THE LAST 41 YEARS — HE SLEEPS IN IT, SWIMS IN IT, AND IS SO GENERALLY ENAMORED OF IT THAT THE LOCALS CALL HIM "UNCLE WIGGY," AND ALWAYS SEEK HIS SAGE ADVICE REGARDING WIGS AND FALSE HAIR OF ANY KIND

JULIUS CAESAR WAS AN INCORRIGIBLE PRACTICAL JOKESTER AND UPON BEING GREETED WITH CRIES OF "HAIL, CAESAR!" WOULD OFTEN STARE BLANKLY, THEN WHEEL AROUND, SAYING "WHERE? WHERE?" TO THE ENDLESS DELIGHT OF HIS SUBJECTS

AN INVISIBLE PUMPKIN WEIGHING A HUNDRED AND TEN POUNDS, BUT WITH *NO MEASUREABLE CIRCUMFERENCE,* WAS GROWN BY HARRY SMYTHE, Warwick, Rhode Island, 1924

ONE OUT OF EVERY SIX CROWS IS ACTUALLY *NOT A CROW*

THE ELEMENT *BORON* DID NOT APPEAR ON THE PERIODIC TABLE UNTIL 1928, WHEN A WEALTHY INDUSTRIALIST NAMED **ERIC LUTTWIDGE BORON**, TO INSURE IMMORTALITY, MADE A SIZABLE FINANCIAL CONTRIBUTION TO THE SCIENTIFIC COMMUNITY. THE CRAVEN WILLINGNESS OF THESE COWARDLY MEN TO CONCOCT THIS BOGUS ELEMENT — *WHICH HAS NEVER EXISTED AT ALL, AND WILL NEVER, EVER EXIST* — DOES NOT SPEAK WELL FOR WESTERN CULTURE AS A WHOLE, OR FOR THESE SO-CALLED *"GUARDIANS OF SCIENCE!"*

AN ELEGANT SILVER CIGARETTE CASE BELONGING TO THE GANGSTER **AL CAPONE** WAS ENGRAVED TO READ: *"WHERE'S THE PARTY?"*

HUNDREDS OF MOLARS DISCOVERED
IN A *"TOOTH GRAVEYARD"* BEAR
A PERFECT RESEMBLANCE
TO DAME EDITH SITWELL

A *JOKE LETTER* SENT TO
GEORGE WASHINGTON DURING
THE WINTER CAMPAIGN OF 1778
MAKES CLEAR REFERENCES TO
JOY-BUZZERS, DRIBBLE GLASSES,
AND WHOOPIE CUSHIONS A *FULL*
HUNDRED YEARS BEFORE ANY OF
THEM WERE INVENTED

A CHILD-SIZED COWBOY HAT, SPURS, AND TINY SIX-SHOOTERS *WERE FOUND IN A 4,000 YEAR-OLD EGYPTIAN TOMB*

THE MANE OF A FULLY-GROWN MALE LION *MAY BE TRIMMED REGULARLY WITH NO ILL-EFFECTS — TO THE LION!*

THE AYATOLLAH KHOMEINI, *THE IRANIAN MUSLIM CLERIC AND REVOLUTIONARY LEADER, WAS A SECRET SLOT-CAR ENTHUSIAST, SPENDING DAYS ON END PERFECTING VARIOUS LAYOUTS AND APPLYING DECALS AND PINSTRIPING TO HIS MINIATURE AUTOMOBILE COLLECTION*

STRICTLY SPEAKING, WEDNESDAY COMES BEFORE TUESDAY

TWO MILLENNIA AGO THE EQUATOR WAS STILL AN ACTUAL LINE, APPROXIMATELY EIGHT YARDS IN WIDTH AND VARYING IN COLOR BY REGION AND TIME OF YEAR! MOST EARLY CARTOGRAPHERS INCLUDED IT ON THEIR MAPS. BY THE EARLY MIDDLE AGES, HOWEVER, MOST OF IT HAD BEEN WORN AWAY BY MOTHER NATURE OR DESTROYED BY MARAUDING TRIBES. NEVERTHELESS CARTOGRAPHERS' HABITS DIE HARD, AND *IT CONTINUES TO APPEAR ON MOST MAPS AND GLOBES TO THIS DAY!*

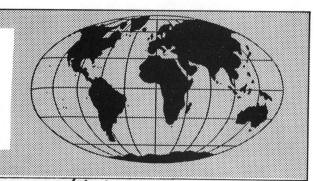

CHINESE FOOD, AS WE KNOW IT, WAS INVENTED *IN ITALY*

THOUGH WEALTHY BEYOND BELIEF **EMPEROR LIN HYUANG TENG** OF CHINA (1530 -1589) WAS UNABLE TO FIND A WIFE BECAUSE OF HIS MEAN DISPOSITION -- IN DESPERATION AT THE AGE OF 55, HE MARRIED A COMMON TOAD, BUT WHEN THE TOAD REFUSED TO BEAR HIM CHILDREN HE WAS UNABLE TO DIVORCE IT BECAUSE OF A STRICT LAW FORBIDDING THE DIVORCE OF AMPHIBIANS *WHICH HE HIMSELF HAD MADE!*

The SOREST LOSER IN THE WORLD!

AT A LOCAL GOLF TOURNAMENT IN HIS HOME STATE OF IOWA, **EVAN PARZUCHOWSKI**, A NOTORIOUSLY SORE LOSER, MANAGED TO COME WITHIN ONE STROKE OF FIRST PLACE ON THE LAST HOLE, WHEN THE WINNING PLAYER DROPPED DEAD -- *OF A MASSIVE STROKE!* IN AN UNPARALLELED PERFORMANCE OF TEAR-FILLED HISTRIONICS PARZUCHOWSKI ARGUED TO THE JUDGES THAT THIS LAST STROKE SHOULD COUNT AS PART OF THE PLAY! SO PERSISTENT WAS HIS NAGGING THAT THE JUDGES RULED IN HIS FAVOR AND *HE TIED FOR FIRST PLACE TO WIN THE TOURNAMENT!*

POKEY,
A SLUG WITH ESP
Sussex, England

FETA CHEESE
IN THE SHAPE
OF NOVELIST
THOMAS MANN

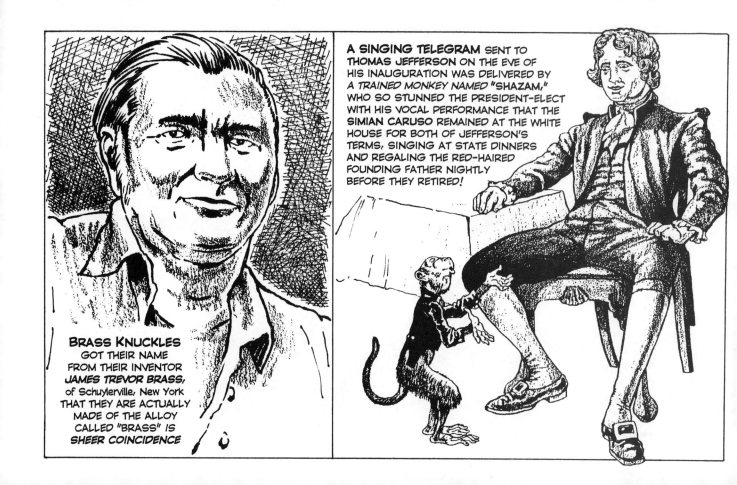

BRASS KNUCKLES GOT THEIR NAME FROM THEIR INVENTOR *JAMES TREVOR BRASS,* of Schuylerville, New York THAT THEY ARE ACTUALLY MADE OF THE ALLOY CALLED "BRASS" *IS SHEER COINCIDENCE*

A SINGING TELEGRAM SENT TO **THOMAS JEFFERSON** ON THE EVE OF HIS INAUGURATION WAS DELIVERED BY A *TRAINED MONKEY NAMED "SHAZAM,"* WHO SO STUNNED THE PRESIDENT-ELECT WITH HIS VOCAL PERFORMANCE THAT THE *SIMIAN CARUSO* REMAINED AT THE WHITE HOUSE FOR BOTH OF JEFFERSON'S TERMS, SINGING AT STATE DINNERS AND REGALING THE RED-HAIRED FOUNDING FATHER NIGHTLY BEFORE THEY RETIRED!

CARROT SHAPED LIKE A POTATO

"SOFT PHANTOM"
WON THE 1957 BELMONT STAKES
— WITHOUT A SINGLE BONE IN ITS BODY!

EMILY PARTON ATTENDED KINDERGARTEN
FOR THE FIRST TIME AT THE HOARY AGE OF 107
— AND FLUNKED OUT!

BO OTT, of Nova Scotia, WHEN HE EMIGRATED TO AMERICA THROUGH ELLIS ISLAND, CRACKED A JOKE TO THE EFFECT THAT THE OFFICIALS WOULD HAVE DIFFICULTY SHORTENING HIS ALREADY SHORT NAME. THE OFFICIAL AT WHOM THIS OFFHANDED CRACK WAS DIRECTED BECAME SO OUTRAGED THAT HE SHORTENED OTT'S NAME BY **TWELVE LETTERS** — THE MAXIMUM ALLOWABLE LIMIT — GIVING THE FORMER MR. OTT A LEGAL NAME OF **NEGATIVE LENGTH!** HE LIVED OUT THE REMAINDER OF HIS DAYS WITH HIS NEGATIVE NAME AND *WAS LEGALLY OBLIGED TO SIGN ALL DOCUMENTS WITH AN ERASER!*

IN MOST OF SCANDINAVIA, *BATS ARE THOUGHT TO BE EXTINCT*

AFRICA DID NOT BECOME A CONTINENT UNTIL 1890

POTATO IN THE SHAPE OF A ROCK FORMATION

THE WORLD'S YOUNGEST TEENAGER!

EWALD WANNSTREN, THE SON OF A BELGIAN MUSICIAN, WAS SO PRECOCIOUS THAT HE BECAME A TEENAGER AT THE MERE AGE OF EIGHT YEARS AND FOUR MONTHS! HE ENTERED HIS TWENTIES ONLY TWO YEARS LATER AND ATTAINED THE AGE OF THIRTY *BY THE TIME HE WAS FOURTEEN!*

THE LAST LAUGH!

BORIUS GRACCHUS, A 19TH CENTURY SWISS PHYSICIAN, WOULD ALWAYS PRESCRIBE A GOOD DOSE OF LAUGHTER AS THE ONLY CURE FOR THE COMMON COLD -- HIS PATIENTS, INVARIABLY THINKING THIS SUGGESTION UTTERLY IDIOTIC, WOULD SCORNFULLY LAUGH IN THE GOOD DOCTOR'S FACE UPON HEARING IT — *THEREBY BECOMING INSTANTLY CURED!*

THE
FLOWERING
VOLCANO,
A PLANT IN THE
CACTUS FAMILY,
THROWS UP
ACRID SMOKE
AND SHOOTS
FLAMING EMBERS
AT PASSERSBY,
*JUST LIKE A
REAL VOLCANO!*

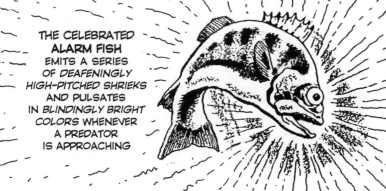

THE CELEBRATED
ALARM FISH
EMITS A SERIES
OF DEAFENINGLY
HIGH-PITCHED SHRIEKS
AND PULSATES
IN *BLINDINGLY BRIGHT*
COLORS WHENEVER
A PREDATOR
IS APPROACHING

THOUGH **PETE PETERSON,** A MECHANIC
IN AMES, IOWA BEARS AN UNCANNY
RESEMBLANCE TO HIS TWIN BROTHER, LEONARD
— *LEONARD LOOKS NOTHING AT ALL LIKE PETE!*

THE BIRDSEED BRIDES

IN THE TOWN OF HUMACAO, PUERTO RICO, IT IS THE LOCAL CUSTOM FOR BRIDES TO WEAR ELABORATE HEADDRESSES MADE ENTIRELY FROM BIRDSEED -- WHILE THE BRIDE AND GROOM WALK IN PROCESSION AROUND THE CHURCH SMALL, GAILY COLORED TROPICAL BIRDS HUNGRILY DEVOUR EVERY LAST BIT OF THE HEADDRESS. ONLY WHEN EVERY LAST SEED HAS BEEN CONSUMED CAN THE RECEPTION AT LAST BEGIN, AT WHICH POINT THE BIRDS, WHICH HAVE BEEN KILLED, PLUCKED, AND DRESSED, ARE SPITROASTED OVER OPEN FIRES, AND SERVED WITH A PIQUANT HERBED DRESSING

THE FAMOUS *BATTLE OF WATERLOO*, LONG CONSIDERED BY HISTORIANS TO BE NAPOLEON'S GREATEST DEFEAT, *ACTUALLY ENDED IN A PERFECT TIE*

CENTRIFUGAL FORCE DID NOT EXIST IN ANY PALPABLE MEASURE UNTIL THE 1910 PASSING OF *HALLEY'S COMET*, WHICH AFFECTED THE MAGNETIC FIELD AROUND THE EARTH'S POLES

PETER AND ARTHUR BOOKMAN,
of Mississippi,
**ARE SIAMESE TWINS
CONNECTED BY
A COMMON
BEARD!**

HE ARRESTED THE CLOUDS!
FOR DARING TO PART AND LET
SUNLIGHT INTERRUPT HIS SPEECH,
ROMAN COMMANDER **FESTUS GAIUS**
(A.D. 326 - 327) ORDERED ALL CLOUDS
IN HIS JURISDICTION TO BE IMPRISONED
FOR TWENTY YEARS! WHEN THEY
REFUSED TO SUBMIT TO HIS DECREE *HE
DOUBLED THEIR SENTENCE!*

THE WORLD'S POLITEST CONDEMNED MAN

UPON LAYING HIS HEAD ON THE CHOPPING BLOCK, JEAN-CLAUDE MALFITE, WHO HAD BEEN SENTENCED TO DEATH FOR HIS INVOLVEMENT IN AN ANARCHIST PLOT AGAINST THE MONARCHY, THANKED HIS EXECUTIONER FOR THE DEED HE WAS ABOUT TO UNDERTAKE, INSISTING THAT HIS HEAD HAD NOT SERVED HIM VERY WELL IN HIS LIFETIME — AFTER ALL IT HAD BROUGHT HIM TO THIS SORRY PASS, HAD IT NOT? — AND IT WAS ONLY A MATTER OF LOGIC THAT HE SHOULD BE SEPARATED FROM IT. HE THEN TIPPED THE EXECUTIONER LAVISHLY, GAVE HIM NUMEROUS PRESENTS AND PRAISED HIM FOR HIS PROFESSIONALISM. THE EXECUTIONER WEPT AT ALL OF THIS, BUT DUTY COMPELLED HIM TO GO THROUGH WITH HIS DEED

DURING THE FIRST AND SECOND ICE AGES, THE SOUTH POLE EXTENDED AS FAR NORTH AS CHICAGO

THE FIRST KNOWN "PIZZAS" WERE HUGE SPHERES OF DOUGH COVERED WITH MOZZARELLA CHEESE AND TOMATO SAUCE THAT OFTEN WEIGHED IN EXCESS OF FIFTY POUNDS! IT WAS NOT UNTIL THE DEVASTATING FLOUR SHORTAGE OF 1880 THAT RESOURCEFUL "PAISANS" BEGAN TO MANUFACTURE THEM IN THE "FLAT" FORM WE KNOW TODAY. NEEDLESS TO SAY, THE FAD CAUGHT ON, AND THEY'VE BEEN MAKING THEM THAT WAY EVER SINCE. — *MANGIA!*

ISAIAH COFFIN, A CONTINENTAL SOLDIER DURING THE AMERICAN REVOLUTION, WAS KILLED AT THE BATTLE OF SARATOGA — AND WAS BURIED IN A COFFIN!

Linkripistalikamanitariumont, AT 28 LETTERS FAR AND AWAY THE LONGEST WORD IN THIS BOOK, HAS NO CORRECT PRONUNCIATION AND IS ENTIRELY MEANINGLESS!

LEMON PEELS,
IF LEFT UNATTENDED
NEAR OPEN WATER,
WILL EVENTUALLY
DEVELOP A SET OF
RUDIMENTARY GILLS
— AND "SWIM" AWAY!

ROCK FORMATION
IN THE SHAPE
OF A POTATO

THE URSINE ABBESS
A COMMON BLACK BEAR
THAT WAS ADOPTED BY A
GROUP OF NUNS
IN THE MONTREAX NUNNERY
WAS TRAINED TO RING
THE BELLS AS A CUB,
AND EVENTUALLY ROSE IN
THE RANKS OF THE ORDER
TO BECOME MOTHER
SUPERIOR OF THE CONVENT
— SHE RULED SUCCESSFULLY
FOR SIXTEEN YEARS
BEFORE BEING *KILLED*
BY POACHERS IN 1549

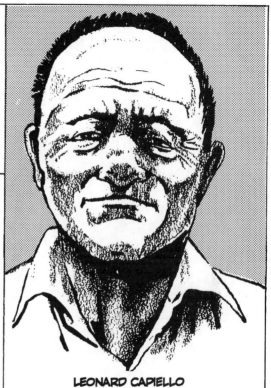

LEONARD CAPIELLO
IS ETHNICALLY 1/3 IRISH,
1/3 ITALIAN, AND
1/3 IRISH-ITALIAN

ZEDEKIAH LIGHTFOOT,
A PRESBYTERIAN MINISTER, WROTE A SERMON A
MINUTE FOR THE LAST *FORTY YEARS* OF HIS LIFE

ED McGRATH, SELF-PROCLAIMED
"PEOPLE'S MAYOR" of Albany, New York,
ROUTINELY RAN AN ENTIRE BILLIARDS
TABLE USING A CUE *NO LARGER
THAN A STANDARD TOOTHPICK*

DURING THE *REVOLUTIONARY WAR* BRITISH FORCES SUFFERED HEAVY LOSSES AT THE HANDS OF **GIANT CANARIES** — SOME AS LARGE AS HORSES! THESE MONSTROUS BIRDS BECAME EXTINCT BY THE 1830'S, BUT DESERVE A SPECIAL PLACE OF HONOR IN AMERICAN HISTORY FOR THEIR NOBLE BEARING AND *THEIR SELFLESS CONTRIBUTIONS TO THE FOUNDING OF THIS GREAT REPUBLIC*

PENNY, A CHIMPANZEE OWNED BY MARY STUARTSON, of Oak Ridge, Indiana, **IS AN EXPERT ON GEORGE WASHINGTON**

THE BARD OF AVON, WILLIAM SHAKESPEARE, WAS ACTUALLY FOUR WOMEN --TWO OF WHOM COULD NEITHER READ NOR WRITE!

COL. MORRIS FINGLE, OF THE CONTINENTAL ARMY, WAS SUCH A NOTORIOUS COWARD THAT HE ONCE NEARLY HIRED SOMEONE TO COMMIT SUICIDE FOR HIM — *BUT THEN CHICKENED OUT!*

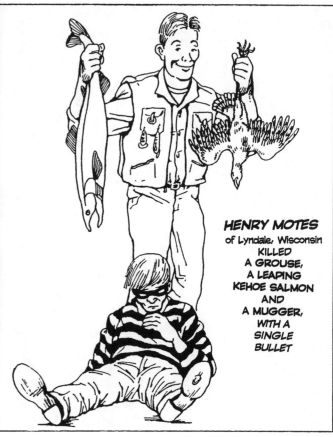

HENRY MOTES
of Lyndale, Wisconsin
KILLED
A GROUSE,
A LEAPING
KEHOE SALMON
AND
A MUGGER,
WITH A
SINGLE
BULLET

THOUGH NOT GENERALLY KNOWN FOR HIS SENSE OF HUMOR, **SENATOR DANIEL WEBSTER** ONCE RELEASED A PAIR OF RABID KANGAROOS INTO THE CAPITOL ROTUNDA TO INFLUENCE VOTING ON A KEY BILL

THE **WORLD'S MOST FINICKY CHEFS**
THE NOTORIOUSLY FASTIDIOUS CHEFS AT LEVIEN-MALRAUX, A POSH RESTAURANT ON THE FRENCH RIVIERA, ARE SO ANXIOUS AND FUSSY ABOUT THE DISHES THEY COOK THAT THEY HAVE BEEN KNOWN TO ACTUALLY BAKE THEMSELVES INTO A PIE OR SOUFFLE SO THAT THEY MAY BETTER OVERSEE ITS PROGRESS **FROM INSIDE THE OVEN!**

THE **MAYA** HAD A SYSTEM OF MATHEMATICS SO ADVANCED THAT THEY THEMSELVES COULD MAKE NEITHER HEAD NOR TAIL OF IT!

A *ZEBRA'S STRIPES* CAN BE EASILY WASHED OFF USING A SOLUTION OF HOUSEHOLD BLEACH AND VINEGAR

BASKETBALL HOOPS ARE NOT CIRCULAR AND HORIZONTAL AS THEY SEEM, BUT ELLIPTICAL AND PITCHED AT A FORTY DEGREE ANGLE -- THEY ONLY APPEAR CIRCULAR BECAUSE OF THE STEEP ANGLE AT WHICH THEY ARE SET. IF THEY WERE IN FACT PERFECTLY CIRCULAR AND HORIZONTAL, SCORING WOULD BE SO EFFORTLESS FOR PROFESSIONAL ATHLETES THAT *MOST GAMES WOULD SOAR UPWARDS OF THOUSANDS AND THOUSANDS OF POINTS, MAKING FOR A RATHER POINTLESS EXHIBITION!*

THE COLOR ORANGE WAS NOT DISCOVERED UNTIL THE INVENTION OF COLOR PHOTOGRAPHY IN 1879

BRAVO! "LORENZO," A NEW YORK CONTEMPORARY PERFORMANCE ARTIST, ONCE WENT FOR A PERIOD OF SEVEN MONTHS **WITHOUT DEFECATING** *— TO CRITICAL AND POPULAR ACCLAIM!*

GERONIMO "HOOPSNAKE" FENTON,
AN APACHE SCOUT, TO AVOID DETECTION, WOULD
SOMERSAULT FOR HOURS THROUGH THE WOODS

A BIRCH TREE
RESEMBLING
A PALM TREE
Biscayne, Florida

THE ENGLISH WORD "CHAIR" HAS BEEN DEFINED WRONG FOR OVER A HUNDRED YEARS -- IT HAS NO CONNECTION WITH THE PIECE OF FURNITURE UPON WHICH PEOPLE SIT, AND HOW IT CAME TO BE MISUSED THAT WAY REMAINS *A COMPLETE MYSTERY*

A COW BEARING A NATURAL BIRTHMARK IN *THE PRECISE SHAPE OF AN ORDINARY ROCK* Berwicka-on-Tweed, England

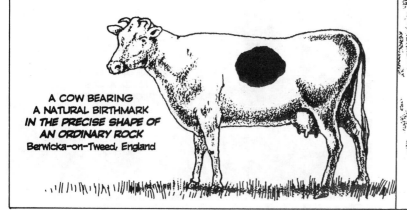

A TEN-THOUSAND YEAR OLD CAVE PAINTING in Rouen, France DEPICTING THAT TOWN'S CURRENT DEPUTY MAYOR, CLAUDE BILDEUX

DAME EMMA SOGAR CLIMBED THE MATTERHORN BAREFOOT AT THE AGE OF SEVENTY-SEVEN — *AND NEVER GOT A SINGLE BLISTER!* SHE CLAIMED THAT THE MEDICINAL PROPERTIES OF FRENCH CHAMPAGNE, IN WHICH SHE SOAKED HER FEET LIBERALLY AT THE END OF EACH DAY'S RIGOROUS CLIMB, WAS ALL THE "FOOTWEAR" SHE REQUIRED!

CHARTRES CATHEDRAL, in Chartres, France, A MARVEL OF HUMAN ENGINEERING, THOUGH IT IS COMPOSED ENTIRELY OF STONES, IS HELD TOGETHER NEAR ITS BASE BY A SINGLE, THREE-INCH SCREW — IF THIS SCREW IS ACCIDENTALLY LOOSENED BY EVEN A QUARTER TURN *THE ENTIRE MAGNIFICENT STRUCTURE WILL COME CRASHING TO THE GROUND!*

DURING WORLD WAR I, *CHEFS UNDER SIEGE* IN A MOUNTAINOUS SECTION OF SWITZERLAND *BUTTERED AN ENTIRE MOUNTAINSIDE* —AND SLID TO SAFETY!

CATS WERE SO REVERED IN ANCIENT EGYPT THAT THEY WERE OFTEN MUMMIFIED A FULL *TWO YEARS BEFORE THEIR DEATH!*

ALBERT WOODS, A BLACKSMITH in Cork, England, *COULD ACTUALLY STAY AWAKE JUST LONG ENOUGH TO HEAR HIMSELF SNORING!*

THE METALLIC MONARCH
DURING A PROLONGED MINERAL SHORTAGE IN HIS COUNTRY, EMPEROR FELIX XVI OF LITHUANIA DECLARED HIMSELF TO BE ALUMINUM, AND WAS SUCCESSFULLY RECYCLED FOUR TIMES BEFORE THE END OF HIS BLOODY REIGN IN 1851

CRICKETS ARE KNOWN TO PERIODICALLY SUFFER *FROM DEPRESSION*

LUKE FIBONNACI,
FAMED MATHEMATICIAN, ARGUED UNTIL HIS DYING DAY THAT THE NUMBERS **TWENTY-TWO** AND **TWENTY-THREE** WERE REVERSED -- HE ALSO BELIEVED THE NUMBER EIGHT WAS A HOAX!

POOH!

THE BROWN WHOOPIE MOTH,
TO DRIVE AWAY LARGE PREDATORS,
MAKES THE UNMISTAKABLE SOUND
OF A DEFLATING WHOOPIE CUSHION

ELVIRA **THURSDAY**,
of Independence, Kansas,
WAS BORN ON A **THURSDAY**,
BAPTIZED ON A **THURSDAY**,
DROPPED OUT OF HIGH SCHOOL ON A **THURSDAY**,
ROBBED HER FIRST BANK ON A **THURSDAY**,
WAS FIRST INCARCERATED ON A **THURSDAY**,
MADE HER FIRST JAILBREAK ON A **THURSDAY**,
AND WAS GUNNED DOWN BY
FEDERAL MARSHALS ON A **THURSDAY!**
SHE WAS BURIED THE FOLLOWING MONDAY

COINS THROWN INTO THE "FOUNTAIN OF ERRORS" in Genoa, Italy, MYSTERIOUSLY REFUSE TO ADD UP TO WHAT THEY SHOULD — THE MORE YOU THROW IN, THE MORE OUTRAGEOUS THE ERROR!

CECIL PORTER, A BOXING INSTRUCTOR, TO BUILD CONFIDENCE IN HIS STUDENTS, WOULD REEL BACK AT THEIR SLIGHTEST TOUCH, THEN PRETEND TO BE DEAD FOR SEVERAL DAYS, ALWAYS CHARGING HIS ELABORATE FUNERALS TO THEIR EXPENSE

ORVILLE AND WILBUR WRIGHT, WHO INVENTED MANNED FLIGHT IN 1903, WERE ACTUALLY NAMED WILBUR AND ORVILLE -- THEIR NAMES WERE SWITCHED BY A FLUSTERED RELATIVE WHEN THEY WERE TEN YEARS OLD AND RATHER THAN OFFEND THE AGED AUNT THEY NEVER REMEDIED IT

EXACTLY ONE-THIRD OF ALL TATTOOS ARE HEREDITARY

AUNT "POOH-POOH" McFLUBBER, A CIRCUS FATLADY IN THE 1920'S, WOULD REGALE AUDIENCES BY SMOTHERING GROWN HOGS WITH HER BODY! SHE WOULD ALSO PINCH THE ROLLS OF FAT IN HER ARMS TO FORM THE LIKENESSES OF ANY ONE OF THE FOUNDING FATHERS -- EXCEPT JAMES MADISON, WHOM SHE DESPISED. SHE ATE HER WEIGHT IN MARSHMALLOWS AND TAFFY EACH DAY, BUT REFUSED TOBACCO — ON ACCOUNT OF HEALTH!

"DIE LUSTIGE NASE,"
MOZART'S LEAST KNOWN OPERATIC WORK,
CONTAINS NO SINGING WHATEVER, BUT
IS A MASTERFUL CHORAL ARRANGEMENT
OF SNEEZES, SNIFFLES, AND SNORTS
ACCORDING TO TRADITION, AT THE END OF
EACH PERFORMANCE THE DIVA IS PRESENTED
WITH A *FRESH LINEN HANDKERCHIEF*

IN SALONIKA, GREECE, LOCAL SWAINS "PROPOSE"
TO THE GIRL OF THEIR CHOICE BY DOODLING HER
FAVORITE FOODS ON A COCKTAIL NAPKIN -- *THE
YOUNG MAN WHOSE DEPICTIONS ARE THE MOST
MOUTH-WATERING IS AWARDED THE GIRL'S HAND
IN MARRIAGE*

HALF OF THE FULLTIME RESIDENTS OF
LAMARR, NEW MEXICO LIVE ELSEWHERE

THOSE DARN VIKINGS!

NEIL ARMSTRONG WAS NOT THE FIRST MAN TO WALK ON THE MOON -- NORSE RUNES TELL THE STORY OF A VIKING LEADER WHO SAILED TO THE MOON VIA NOVA SCOTIA *SOMETIME IN THE ELEVENTH CENTURY*

MARKINGS ON THE VENTRAL SIDE OF A BALEEN WHALE WASHED UP ON THE COAST OF SCOTLAND THAT SPELLED THE POLITICAL SLOGAN *"I LIKE IKE"* — *IN 1852!*

JAMES WINCHESTER MERIWETHER (1798-1884) WAS ELECTED TO THE U.S. HOUSE OF REPRESENTATIVES *FOR SEVEN SUCCESSIVE TWO-YEAR TERMS IN THE SPACE OF A SINGLE DECADE* BEFORE IT WAS DISCOVERED THAT THIS WAS *CHRONOLOGICALLY IMPOSSIBLE*

A *GERANIUM* GROWING OUT OF A MAN'S ELBOW, Montreal, Canada

MAKE WOMB FOR GREATNESS

THE PRECOCIOUSNESS OF ALBERTO EMMANUEL (1533 – 1604), A PADUAN NOBLEMAN, WAS SO WELL-KNOWN THROUGHOUT HIS COUNTRY THAT HE WAS AWARDED THE DEGREE OF DOCTOR OF ARTS AND SCIENCES FROM THE UNIVERSITY OF GENOA — *WHILE STILL IN HIS MOTHER'S WOMB!*

A FULLY-GROWN
GRIZZLY BEAR
SO SMALL
IT COULD FIT
INSIDE
A *CHILD'S SHOE*

CHILDREN IN
THE BASMATI TRIBE
of Eastern Pakistan
ARE FORBIDDEN
TO SNEEZE
UNDER ANY
CIRCUMSTANCES

SELVERT,
THIRD SON OF
THE ARCHDUKE
OF BURGUNDY,
AS A CHILDISH
EASTER PRANK
SWALLOWED A
LIVE RABBIT WHOLE
— THEN HOPPED
HIMSELF TO DEATH
BEFORE HORRIFIED
FRIENDS AND RELATIVES!

A WORKING XEROX MACHINE WAS FOUND IN THE *RUINS OF POMPEII*

ADMIRAL DOOHEY, COMMANDER OF THE BRITISH NAVY DURING THE LATTER YEARS OF QUEEN VICTORIA'S REIGN WOULD REGALE HIS CHIEF OFFICERS AT EVERY AVAILABLE OPPORTUNITY **BY DOING A STANDING BACKFLIP IN FULL DRESS UNIFORM.** WHEN HER MAJESTY LEARNED OF THE ADMIRAL'S OPEN BUFFOONERY SHE SUMMONED HIM TO BUCKINGHAM PALACE -- BUT SO TAKEN WAS THE OCTOGENARIAN MONARCH WITH THE ADMIRAL'S LOW STUNT THAT SHE COAXED HIM INTO GIVING HER PRIVATE LESSONS IN THIS "SECRET ART" *— NEARLY BREAKING HER NECK -- AND SENDING SHOCK WAVES THROUGHOUT THE WORLD'S FINANCIAL MARKETS!*

SPUDS AND ALE!

VETERAN HORSE JOCKEY BILLY COBBLER SINCE CHILDHOOD HAD AN OUTSIZED APPETITE FOR HORSEMEAT, AND LIKED NOTHING BETTER THAN TO DINE ON A FRESH HORSE STEAK SMOTHERED IN ONIONS -- ALWAYS SERVED WITH HEAPING MOUNDS OF SNOWY MASHED POTATOES AND COPIOUS DRAUGHTS OF FROTHY ALE. THE WILY COBBLER WOULD REPORTEDLY TELL HIS TERRIFIED MOUNTS OF HIS STRANGE "TASTE" PRIOR TO A RACE -- AND WARN THEM THAT IF THEY DIDN'T PERFORM WELL HE WOULD SEE TO IT THAT THEY "JOINED HIM AT TABLE" THAT NIGHT! *THUS WHENEVER HIS HORSE BEGAN TO FLAG DURING A RACE, NEARBY JOCKEYS COULD HEAR COBBLER CRUELLY GOADING THE BEAST WITH HIS TRADEMARK CRY OF "SPUDS AND ALE! SPUDS AND ALE!"* UNTIL THE CHASTENED CREATURE, GOGGLE-EYED WITH TERROR, PULLED AHEAD OF THE PACK!

A COMMON SPECIES OF **FRESHWATER CLAM** POSSESSES THE ABILITY TO COUNT TO THE NUMBER FOUR

STEE-RIKE!!

LOUIS SCHENCK, OR *"OLD GASSY"* AS HE WAS CALLED, WAS AN UMPIRE DURING THE 1920'S WHO SUFFERED FROM SUCH HARROWINGLY PAINFUL INTESTINAL CRAMPS THAT HE OFTEN PUNCTUATED HIS CALLS AT THE PLATE WITH LOUD **WHOOPS AND CRIES** -- *MANY TIMES JABBING THE AIR OR CONTORTING HIS BODY TO RELIEVE THE SEARING PAIN.* OTHER UMPIRES FOUND THAT APING SCHENCK'S GAS-INSPIRED THEATRICS PROVED A TERRIFIC CROWD PLEASER — *AND THESE SHENANIGANS REMAIN WITH US TODAY AS A SEEMINGLY INDISPENSIBLE PART OF THE GAME*

SIAMESE
CATS

GEORGETTE MORRISON, of Merrick, Texas, SUFFERED FROM TERRIFIC COUGHING SPELLS ALL HER LIFE. AT THE AGE OF 43, HOWEVER, AFTER GREAT DIFFICULTY, SHE *COUGHED UP A SILVER SPOON* WHICH HER OWN GRANDMOTHER HAD SWALLOWED DURING THE CIVIL WAR IN AN EFFORT TO KEEP IT FROM A UNION SOLDIER WHO HAD ENTERED HER HOME! MISS MORRISON WAS CURED INSTANTLY -- BUT TRAGICALLY, THE PHYSICIAN ATTENDING HER DURING THIS DIFFICULT EPISODE WAS HIMSELF *THE VERY SAME UNION SOLDIER'S GRANDSON!* ON SEEING THE ELUSIVE PIECE OF SILVERWARE HE QUICKLY SNATCHED IT UP, EXCUSED HIMSELF, AND FLED THE PREMISES, *NEVER TO BE SEEN AGAIN!*

THOUGH THE CHARMING FAIRYTALE OF **GOLDILOCKS AND THE THREE BEARS** HAS BEEN TOLD OVER AND OVER TO COUNTLESS GENERATIONS OF ADORING LISTENERS, THE SIMPLE FACTS OF THE MATTER CONTINUALLY POINT TO THE INVOLVEMENT OF BUT A SINGLE BEAR

THE ENGLISH NAME NANCY MEANS "STICK 'EM UP!" *IN SWAHILI*

THE RENOWNED 15TH CENTURY FLEMISH PAINTER, *PIETER BRUEGHEL*, LIVED HIS ENTIRE ADULT LIFE IN A HOUSE BUILT UPON A GIANT ANTHILL AND CLAIMED TO KNOW EACH AND EVERY ONE OF ITS FORTY-THOUSAND INHABITANTS *BY NAME*

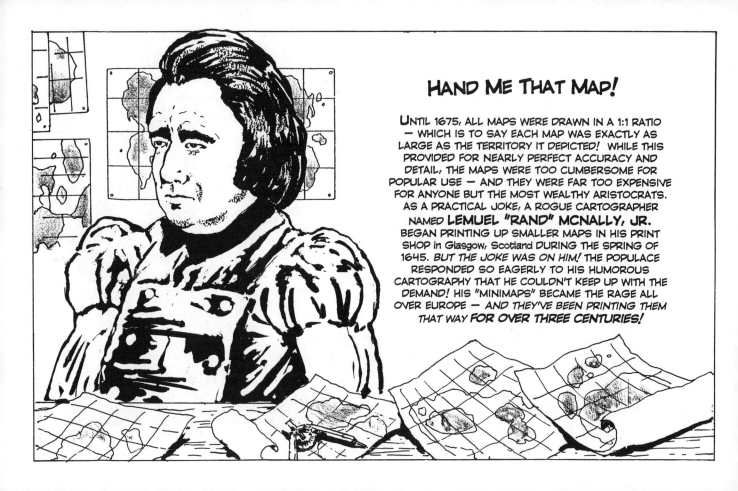

HAND ME THAT MAP!

UNTIL 1675, ALL MAPS WERE DRAWN IN A 1:1 RATIO — WHICH IS TO SAY EACH MAP WAS EXACTLY AS LARGE AS THE TERRITORY IT DEPICTED! WHILE THIS PROVIDED FOR NEARLY PERFECT ACCURACY AND DETAIL, THE MAPS WERE TOO CUMBERSOME FOR POPULAR USE — AND THEY WERE FAR TOO EXPENSIVE FOR ANYONE BUT THE MOST WEALTHY ARISTOCRATS. AS A PRACTICAL JOKE, A ROGUE CARTOGRAPHER NAMED **LEMUEL "RAND" MCNALLY, JR.** BEGAN PRINTING UP SMALLER MAPS IN HIS PRINT SHOP in Glasgow, Scotland DURING THE SPRING OF 1645. *BUT THE JOKE WAS ON HIM!* THE POPULACE RESPONDED SO EAGERLY TO HIS HUMOROUS CARTOGRAPHY THAT HE COULDN'T KEEP UP WITH THE DEMAND! HIS "MINIMAPS" BECAME THE RAGE ALL OVER EUROPE — AND THEY'VE BEEN PRINTING THEM THAT WAY *FOR OVER THREE CENTURIES!*

THE FAMOUS
TREE-CLIMBING APES
of Borneo and Sumatra
EXPLODE AT ALTITUDES
EXCEEDING EIGHTY FEET

**A DUNG
BEETLE**
IS SMARTER
THAN A LION

THE MATING CALL
OF THE MARYLAND
STRIPED THRUSH
SOUNDS REMARKABLY
*LIKE AN EXPLODING
OIL TANKER*

The Crooning Trout of New Hampshire

BROWN TROUT IN THE STREAMS NEAR BARRE STATE FOREST IN SOUTHERN NEW HAMPSHIRE POSSESS THE MYSTERIOUS ABILITY TO MIMIC SONGS SUNG OR WHISTLED BY FISHERMEN OR HIKERS IN THE AREA -- PEOPLE BY THE THOUSANDS HAVE STOOD ON THE BANKS OF THESE STREAMS TO HEAR THESE EXTRAORDINARY FISH "PERFORM" POP TUNES AND JAZZ STANDARDS IN EXCHANGE FOR NO MORE THAN A PIECE OF STALE BREAD OR WRIGGLING WORM! SO AFFECTING ARE THE VOICES OF THESE *CELESTIAL TROUT* THAT ONCE THEY ARE HEARD EVEN THE MOST HARDENED AND JADED OF MISANTHROPES HAVE BEEN REDUCED TO **BLUBBERING WRECKS**, SELLING ALL THEIR BELONGINGS AND SPENDING *THE REST OF THEIR DAYS IN RAPT BLISS AT THE* ***GLORIOUS WARBLINGS*** OF THESE SINGULAR SUBMARINE CREATURES!

UNTIL *1762* THE MONTH OF SEPTEMBER POSSESSED NOT LESS THAN SIXTY-ONE DAYS — MAKING IT THE LONGEST MONTH IN THE YEAR! ONLY AT THE PERSISTENT SUGGESTION OF THE CRAFTY **BENJAMIN FRANKLIN** — WHO GREEDILY LOBBIED FOR A TWELVE MONTH YEAR IN ORDER THAT HIS LUCRATIVE POOR RICHARD'S ALMANACK WOULD INCREASE ITS REVENUES STILL FURTHER — WAS THE SITUATION REMEDIED. DR. FRANKLIN PROPOSED THE NOVEL SOLUTION OF SPLITTING SEPTEMBER INTO TWO SEPARATE MONTHS — ONE OF THIRTY DAYS, AND A SECOND OF THIRTY-ONE DAYS. THE FIRST WOULD NATURALLY RETAIN THE NAME SEPTEMBER, WHILE THE SECOND WOULD SPORT THE AS-YET UNHEARD APPELLATION OF "OCTOBER." **TWO CENTURIES LATER IT SEEMS ALMOST IMPOSSIBLE TO IMAGINE AN AUTUMN WITHOUT IT!**

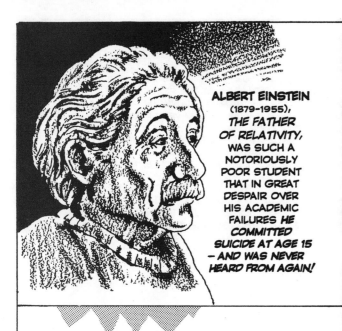

ALBERT EINSTEIN (1879-1955), *THE FATHER OF RELATIVITY,* WAS SUCH A NOTORIOUSLY POOR STUDENT THAT IN GREAT DESPAIR OVER HIS ACADEMIC FAILURES *HE COMMITTED SUICIDE AT AGE 15* – AND WAS NEVER *HEARD FROM AGAIN!*

EACH OF THE ENTRIES IN THIS BOOK, EXCEPTING THIS ONE, ARE *WITHOUT* A SINGLE EXCEPTION, ENTIRELY UNTRUE

YOGURT IS MYSTERIOUSLY INEDIBLE TO ANYONE WHO HAS TRAVELED IN SPACE

About the Author

ERIC METAXAS GRADUATED YALE UNIVERSITY IN 1984 WHERE HE EDITED THE *YALE RECORD*, THE NATION'S OLDEST COLLEGE HUMOR MAGAZINE. HIS HUMOR WRITING HAS APPEARED IN *THE NEW YORK TIMES MAGAZINE* AND *THE ATLANTIC*. AS HEADWRITER FOR THE CRITICALLY ACCLAIMED RABBIT EARS PRODUCTIONS, MR. METAXAS WROTE OVER **TWENTY** CHILDREN'S STORIES -- ALL OF WHICH CAN BE HEARD ACROSS THE COUNTRY WEEKLY ON *PRI'S RABBIT EARS RADIO*. HIS MOST RECENT BOOKS ARE *THE BIRTHDAY ABC* AND *THE WILD RIDE OF MISS IMPALA GEORGE!*

About The Artist

MARC DENNIS DID NOT GRADUATE YALE UNIVERSITY. HE'S A PAINTER, ILLUSTRATOR, GRAPHIC & TEXTILE DESIGNER AND ART TEACHER. HE CURRENTLY LIVES AND WORKS IN NEW YORK CITY.